PLAY LEARN COOK and HAVE FUN

by: Chef Jazz Jazz

DULCIA ALEXANDER

PLAY LEARN COOK and HAVE FUN

Copyright © 2024 by Dulcia Alexander

ISBN: 978-1962497916(hc)
ISBN: 978-1962497909(sc)
ISBN: 978-1962497923(e)

The Reading Glass Books
(888) 420-3050
www.readingglassbooks.com
fulfillment@readingglassbooks.com

Table of Contents

Jello Sundae With Whipped Cream

Ingredients:

- 1 pack of red Jello
- 1 pack of orange jello
- 1 pack of green jello
- 1 pack of yellow jello

Directions:

1. Pour the various flavored Jello in separate bowls.
2. For each flavored jello add boiling water to the gelatin mix and then stir in cold water and place in the refrigerator for about four hours or until firm.
3. Place the Oreos on top of the jello.
4. Add vanilla ice cream on top of the Oreos.
5. Garnish each side with two rice krispies.
6. Drizzle chocolate and strawberry syrup on top.
7. Repeat same steps for each flavor.

3

English Muffins Pizza

Ingredients:

- English Muffins
- 1 cup of pizza sauce
- ¼ cup of mozzarella cheese
- ¼ cup of cheddar cheese
- 5 pieces of pepperoni
- ¼ teaspoon of oregano
- 1 teaspoon of basil
- 1 pinch of parsley (chopped finely)

Directions:

1. Preheat oven to 350.
2. Cut the English muffin in half.
3. Add your pizza sauce to your English muffin. Spread evenly with the back side of a spoon.
4. Add a pinch of oregano or basil. (optional).
5. Sprinkle mozzarella cheese and cheddar cheese.
6. Add pepperoni or your desired pizza toppings.
7. Bake for about 10-20 minutes in the oven or place in the air fryer for 5-10 minutes.

Then cool, cut and enjoy!

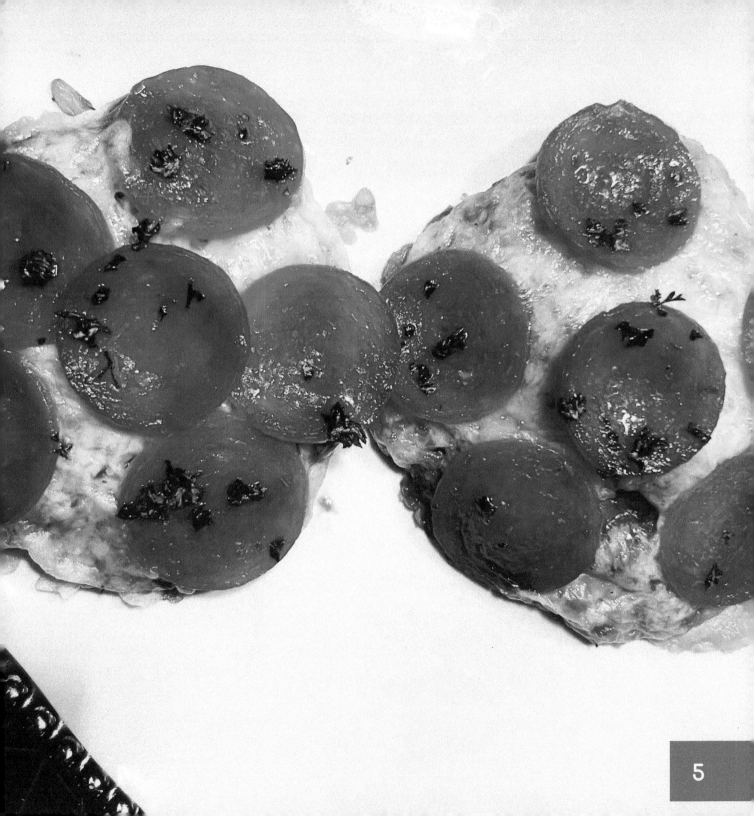

Cucumber, Tomatoes, Raisins and Cranberry Salad

Ingredients:

- 2 cucumbers (chopped into small cubes)
- 2 tomatoes (cut in cubes)
- ¼ red onions
- ¼ cup of cranberries
- ¼ cup of raisins
- 1 teaspoon of olive oil
- 1 tablespoon of sugar
- 1 teaspoon of white vinegar
- 1 pinch of black pepper

Directions:

1. Place cucumber, tomatoes, and onion into a large bowl.
2. Add olive oil, sugar and white vinegar to the bowl.
3. Mix well.
4. Place the lettuce on a dinner plate then add the cucumber, tomatoes and onion mix on top.
5. Finally garnish with back pepper, raisins and cranberries.

Chill, server and enjoy!

Cinnamon Honey Pineapple Salad

Ingredients:

- 1 whole pineapple
- 1 teaspoon of cinnamon
- 1 cup of strawberries (sliced)
- ¼ cup of cherries
- 2 tablespoon of honey
- Flower shapr cookie cutter

Directions:

1. Cut Pineapple into circlers shape then use cookie cutter to shape into flower.
2. Place on a plate neatly.
3. Sprinkle cinnamon and drizzle honey on top of pineapple.
4. Add the cherry in the center of the star shape pineapples.
5. Chill then serve.

Mini Chocolate Bagel Blast

Ingredients:

- 3 mini bagels
- 1 cup of cream cheese
- ¼ cup chocolate syrup
- 1 container of chocolate icing or whipped cream

Directions:

1. Cut the bagel in half.
2. Combine cream cheese and chocolate syrup. (mix together well).
3. Apply the mixture to all halves of the bagel evenly.
4. Add chocolate icing and or whipped cream on top
5. Drizzle chocolate syrup on top.

Serve and enjoy!

Egg Salad Toast

Ingredients:

- 4 boil eggs
- 1 pinch of salt
- 1 pinch of black pepper
- 1 tablespoon of mayonnaise
- 1 pinch of dill
- 2 celery stalks
- ½ of green bell or sweet pepper
- 4 slices of bread
- A flower cookie cutter

Directions:

Egg salad:

1. Mash eggs well with a fork, then add mayo, black pepper, salt and dill.
2. Place the pieces of bread on a clean surface, then use the cookie cutter to form the flower shape.
3. Spread the egg salad on top of the bread.
4. Cut the celery stalks into long strips (the stem of the flower) and place them at the center of the bread.
5. Cut the sweet peppers into small circles and place them on the or on top of the sandwiches.

Enjoy your Flower Toast egg salad sandwiches

13

Gummy Lemonade

Ingredients:

- 5 cups of water
- 1 tablespoon of lemon juice
- 1 cup of sugar
- 1 gummy shaped tray
- 1 assorted color

Directions:

1. Add water to a pitcher or container.
2. Add lemon juice and sugar and mix well.
3. Place it in the refrigerator until its cold.

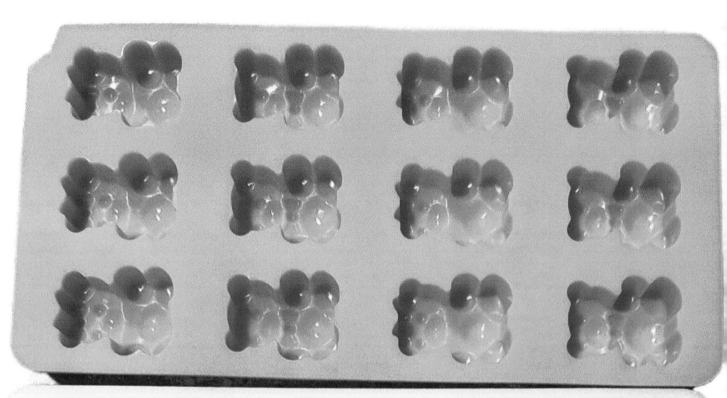

Gummy Ice

Directions:

1. Add water to the gummy-shaped tray then add food coloring of your choice to the water in the gummy- shaped tray.
2. Put the tray in the freezer for 2-3 hours.
3. Add gummy cubes to your drink and enjoy!

Peanut Butter Jelly Squares

Ingredients:

- 4 slices of bread (not toasted)
- ½ cup of grape jelly
- ½ cup of strawberry jelly
- 1 cup of peanut butter

Directions:

1. Place the 4 slices of bread on a flat surface.
2. Using the back of a spoon, spread 1 slice of bread with grape jelly, 1 slice of strawberry jelly and the last two slices spread with peanut butter.
3. Stack in four with jelly on top then peanut butter on the bottom.
4. Then cut off edges and cut horizontally in the stack layers.

Dress up Barbie Ice Cream

Ingredients:

- 3 scoops of strawberry ice cream
- I ripe banana (split)
- 2 tablespoons of strawberry syrup
- I teaspoon of pink editable glitter
- I can of pink editable spray
- 6 strawberry cream cookies

Directions:

1. Cut the banana into four then spray with editable pink spray.
2. Place ice cream in a bowl then add the bananas to each end of the bowl.
3. Add strawberry cream cookies around the rim of the bowl.

Garnish:

Add whip cream
Add mamba magic pink candy sticks
Drizzle with strawberry syrup

Strawberry Bagel Blast

Ingredients:

- 1 large bagel
- ¼ cup of strawberry cream cheese
- ¼ cup of fresh strawberries
- 2 tablespoons of strawberry syrup
- Whip cream
- 1 teaspoon of edible pink glitter

Directions:

1. Cut the bagel in half.
2. Apply cream cheese to both sides of the bagel.
3. Mix together strawberries and strawberry syrup.
4. Spread the mixture to both sides of the bagel.
5. Apply whip cream.
6. Sprinkle the pink editable glitter on top of the whip cream.
7. Drizzle strawberry syrup on top.

Then serve and enjoy!

Strawberry Milkshake

Ingredients:

- 1 cup of milk
- 2 scoops of strawberry ice cream
- 1 cup of fresh strawberries
- 2 teaspoon of strawberry syrup
- 2 french vanilla pirouette sticks (pepperidge brand)
- Whip cream
- Red editable glitter

Directions:

1. Place ice cream, milk, strawberries and strawberry syrup into a blender for 1 minute.
2. Pour the mixture into a glass.
3. Garnish with whipped cream and your French vanilla sticks.
4. Sprinkle the edible glitter on top.

Flowers Fruit Salad

Ingredients:

- Watermelon cut into chunks
- 1 cup of cantaloupe
- 1 cup of pineapple
- 1 cup of grapes
- 1 cup of blueberries
- 1 cup of honey dew
- 1 tablespoon of lemon juice
- Flower cookie cutter

Directions:

1. Cut each fruit (except grapes and blueberries) into flowers with your cookie cutter.
2. Place each fruit on a platter.
3. Separate your flower cut out fruits from your grapes and blueberries.
4. Place each flower "cut out" equally apart then place the blueberries or grapes in the center of the fruit flower.
5. Make a mixture of honey and lemon juice and glaze it on top of all your fruit.
6. Chill in the refrigerator and Enjoy your Fruity Flowers.

Avocado Boiled Egg Toast

Ingredients:

- 1 large avocado (sliced)
- 2 boiled eggs (cut in circles or roundly)
- 1 teaspoon of mayonnaise (optional)
- 1 teaspoon of mild salsa
- 1 slice of pita bread

Directions:

1. Slice the avocado then add mayonnaise to the toasted pita bread.
2. Place the avocado slices on the toasted bread in a circular shape then add the boiled eggs and salsa in the middle.

Serve and Enjoy

29

Strawberry Doughnut Delight

Ingredients:

- 2 glazed donuts
- 1 cup of fresh strawberries
- ¼ cup of strawberry syrup
- 1 scoop of ice cream
- 1 can of whipped cream
- 1 pink edible glitter or brew dust

Directions:

1. Cut the donut in half.
2. Apply ice cream in between the donut.
3. Mix the strawberries and the strawberry syrup together.
4. Add the strawberry mixture in between both donuts.
5. Apply whipped cream to your desire and drizzle with strawberry syrup and sprinkle the pink editable glitter or brew dust on top.

Barbie World Cheesecake

Ingredients:

- 1 (24.3oz) of no bake cheesecake (any brand)
- 1 Graham cracker crust pie shell
- ½ cup of powdered sugar
- 1 cup of sour cream
- Pink food coloring

Directions:

1. Place the container of no-bake cheesecake into a bowl.
2. Add ½ cup of sour cream into the bowl.
3. Add pink food coloring until the mixture is your desired color of pink.
4. Stir all the ingredients together until you get a thick pink filling.
5. Evenly spread the filling into the graham cracker crust until its smooth all around.

Glaze topping:

1. Add ½ cup of powdered sugar and sour cream to a bowl.
2. Apply the pink food coloring into the mixture until it's a hot pink color.
3. Mix all ingredients together until it becomes a thick glaze.
4. Spread evenly on top of the cheesecake mixture in the graham cracker crust pie shell.
5. Garnish with whipped cream and strawberry syrup.
6. Place the pie into the freezer and allow it to chill for 3-4 hours.

Serve Chill and Enjoy!

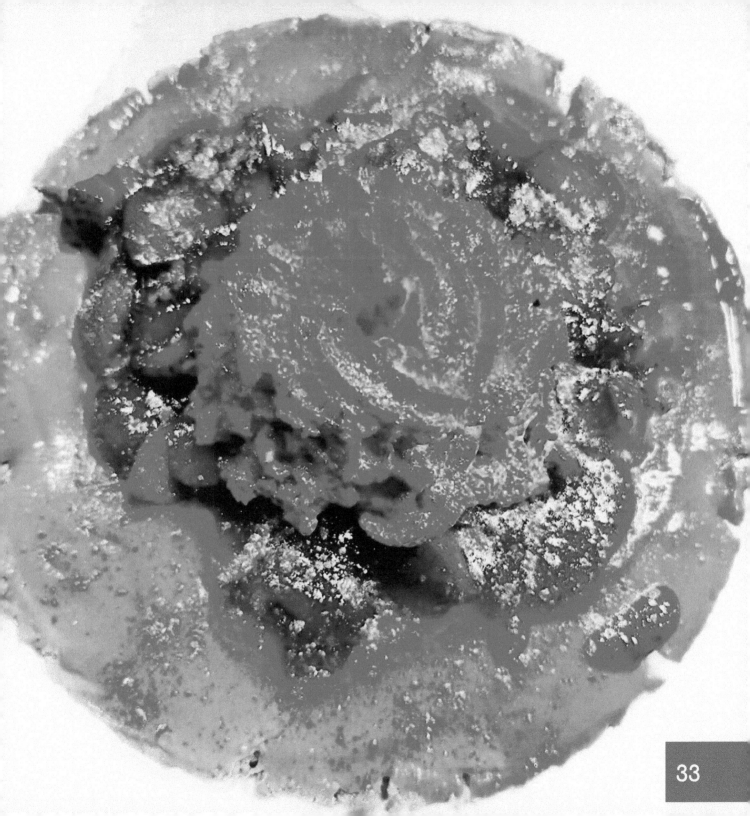

33

Mermaid Drink

Ingredients:

- 1 glass of pineapple juice
- 1 teaspoon of blue curacao non-alcoholic
- 1 cherry

Directions:

1. Use a plastic wine glass filled with pineapple juice.
2. Add a teaspoon of blue curacao DO NOT STIR.
3. Add cherry on top.
4. Garnish your drink with a small sized pineapple fruit cut into a little piece.

Chill and Enjoy

Triple Chocolate Ice Cream Sandwich

Ingredients:

- 2 large chocolate chipped cookies
- 1 scoop of vanilla ice cream
- 1 teaspoon of chocolate syrup
- Strawberry syrup
- 1 cup of fresh strawberries
- Whipped cream

Directions:

1. Place the cookies on a flat surface.
2. Place one scoop of the ice cream in between the cookies to form a sandwich.
3. Place it back in the freezer for 1 hour.
4. Mix strawberries and syrup together.
5. Pour the mixture over the sandwich then add whipped cream and drizzle chocolate syrup.
6. Garnish the top with 2 chocolate stick.

Serve and enjoy!

Chocolate Milkshake

Ingredients:

- 3 scoops of chocolate ice cream
- 1 cup of milk
- ¼ cup of chocolate syrup
- Whipped cream
- 2 chocolate bars (break into sticks)
- 6 individual chocolate teddy grahams

Directions:

1. Place ice cream, milk and syrup into a small blender for 5 seconds.
2. Pour the mixture into a cup.
3. Garnish with whipped cream and chocolate syrup.
4. Add the chocolate bar sticks at each end.
5. Add teddy grahams surrounding the rim of the cup.

Serve and Enjoy!

Mickey Mouse Sundae

Ingredients:

- 5 small m&m cookies
- 2 scoops of vanilla ice cream
- 10 pieces of m&m candy
- Chocolate syrup
- Whipped cream

Directions:

1. Place 2 cookies in the bottom of a glass.
2. Add 1 scoop of ice cream (this is the start of a layers.)
3. Crumble up 1 cookie then add chocolate syrup and then a scoop of ice cream.
4. Then add more syrup and whipped cream.
5. Lastly add two cookies to each side, garnish with whipped cream, chocolate syrup and remaining cookie crumbled.

Chocolate Sundae

Ingredients:

- 4 scoop Chocolate Ice cream
- 1 Cup crush Oreo cookies
- 2 single Oreo cookie (not crushed)
- 1/2 cup Cholate syrup
- whip cream
- 2 white Cholate bar

Directions:

1. Place 2 scoop Ice cream into a clear glass
2. Then add Chocolate syrup and crushed Oreo cookies
3. Next, add 2 more scoop Ice cream then remain of crush Oreo then whip cream and dissle syrup and place the two Oreo cookies in Both side for mickey CAS
4. Place Chocolate bar right below the Cookie then enjoy!!

Mango Spinach Salad

Ingredients:

- 1 large bowl of spinach (finely chopped)
- ¼ cup of all natural maple syrup
- 2 ripe mangos (chopped)
- 2 tablespoon of almonds (finely chopped)
- 2 teaspoons of pecans (finely chopped)
- ¼ cup of dried cranberries (diced)

Directions:

1. Place finely chopped spinach into a large bowl.
2. Add the maple syrup to the bowl and mix the ingredients together.
3. Then add mangos, pecans, almonds and dried cranberries for garnish.

Maple Carrot Salad

Ingredients:

- 5 Cups of shredded carrots
- ¼ cup of maple syrup
- ¼ cup of dried cranberries
- 2 tablespoons of raisins
- ½ cup of pineapple (chopped finely)
- 4 pineapple ring circle

Directions:

1. Place carrots into a large bowl.
2. Add cranberries, raisins and pineapples.
3. Add your maple syrup and mix everything together.
4. (Optional) place salad in-between pineapple circle.

Chill it and then enjoy.

Avocado Cheese Rolls

Ingredients:

- 6 slices of white bread
- 2 avocados mashed
- 6 teaspoons of mayonnaise
- 1 teaspoon of yellow food coloring
- 1 cup of shredded swiss cheese

Directions:

1. Place avocado in a bowl with mayo mix together until it becomes fluffy texture.
2. In a separate bowl add the shredded cheese with mayonnaise and food coloring until the color changes.
3. Lay out your bread and cut off the edges on all sides.
4. Layer each piece of bread with the avocado mixture.
5. On another slice of bread layer the cheese.
6. Then roll each piece (should be cylinder shaped)
7. Then cut 1 ½ inches forming pinwheels.

Serve and enjoy!

49

Rainbow Cheese Roll

Ingredients:

- 8 slices of bread not toasted
- 8 tablespoons of mayo
- 8 cups of white shredded cheese
- 4 different color food coloring

Directions:

1. Obtain 4 different bowls.
2. Add 2 tablespoons of mayo and 2 cups of shredded cheese to each bowl.
3. Then add your food colorings separately to each bowl.
4. Mix each bowl well.
5. Layer each piece of bread with shredded cheese mixture separately.
6. Roll each piece (in a cylinder shape).
7. Cut 1 ½ inches forming pinwheels.

Serve and Enjoy!

Barbie Lemonade

Ingredients:

- 1 ½ cup of water
- 2 tablespoon of lemon juice
- 2 tablespoon of sugar
- ½ cup of cranberry juice
- 1 teaspoon of pink editable glitter or brew dust

Directions:

1. Obtain a large Glass
2. Mix water, lemon juice and sugar reaching halfway point of the glass.
3. Add cranberry juice and the pink glitter or brew dust to the remaining half of the pitcher.

Garnish:

1. Obtain a glass.
2. On a small plate add sugar and pink brew dust.
3. Mix the sugar and pink dust together.
4. Wet the rim of the glass with simple sugar and then take your glass and coat the rim with the simple sugar.
5. Then place the rim of the glass circularly around the sugar and pink brew dust creating a pink glittery rim.

Chocolate Delight Sundae

Ingredients:

- 3 baby chocolate Bundt's
- 2 scoops of ice cream
- ½ cup of chocolate teddy grahams
- Whipped cream
- Chocolate syrup
- 2 white chocolate bars
- 2 Oreo cookies

Directions:

1. Place the baby Bundt's into a small bowl.
2. Then place the 2 scoops of ice cream and the teddy graham on top.
3. Add your chocolate syrup and whipped cream.
4. Garnish with a chocolate syrup drizzle and place the oreo and chocolate bars on top.

Fruit Parfait

Ingredients:

- 3 cups of vanilla yogurt
- 2 slices of cake
- 1 cup of strawberries
- 1 cup of blueberries
- ¼ cup of granola
- 3 tablespoons of strawberry syrup

Directions:

1. Obtain a glass.
2. Place 1 cup of yogurt at the bottom of the glass.
3. Place a piece of cake on top of the yogurt.
4. Add strawberries and the strawberry syrup.
5. Continue the layer adding another cup of vanilla yogurt then adding blueberries on top.
6. Add the granola and another slice of cake.
7. Lastly add another cup of vanilla yogurt, granola and strawberry syrup.
8. Garnish the top with extra strawberry syrup and granola.

Chicken Salad Flower Sandwich

Ingredients:

- 3 different food coloring
- 3 cups of finely chopped chicken breast
- 3 tablespoons of mayo
- 1 pinch of black pepper
- 1 tablespoon of celery finely chopped
- 1 tablespoon of finely chopped onion

Directions:

1. Place all ingredients into a large bowl and mix well. (Except the food coloring)
2. In a separate bowl place the mixture you created (Chicken salad) and the food coloring.
3. Obtain 6 slices of bread 2 stalks of celery and 1 flower shaped cookie cutter.
4. Use the flower shaped cookie cutter to cut the bread into flower shapes.
5. Add half of the chicken salad on top of the bread neatly (forming a sandwich).
6. Cut your celery into smaller stalks and place at the center of your flower shaped sandwiches.

Avocado Tuna Salad

Ingredients:

- 1 can of tuna
- 1 cup of corn
- 1 cup of avocadoes cut in cubes
- ¼ cup of tomatoes
- ¼ cup of cucumbers
- 1 tablespoon of red onions
- 1 tablespoon of chopped parsley
- 1 tablespoon of yellow mustard
- 1 pinch of salt
- 1 tablespoon of vinegar
- 1 pinch of black pepper
- 1 teaspoon of lime juice

Directions:

1. Place all ingredients into a large bowl.
2. Then add the salt, mustard, vinegar and pepper.
3. Mix well and then serve.

Peach Parfait Yogurt

Ingredients:

- 2 slices of vanilla cake
- 2 cups of peach yogurt
- 1 cup of sliced peaches
- ¼ cup of peach jelly
- ¼ cup of granola
- 1 cup slice fresh peaches

Directions:

1. Place one cup of peach yogurt into a glass.
2. Then add a piece of cake on top of the yogurt.
3. Then add again another cup of yogurt.
4. Add the peaches and peach jelly on top of the 2nd layer.
5. On your third layer you're going to add another cup of peach yogurt and another slice of cake.
6. Garnish with a slice of peach and sprinkle some granola on top.

Serve and Enjoy!

Pineapple Sunset Drink

Ingredients:

- 2 cups of pineapple juice
- ½ cup of soda water
- 1 teaspoon of red grenadine

Directions:

1. Obtain a glass.
2. Fill your glass 2/3 of the way full with pineapple juice.
3. Fill the remaining with soda water.
4. Add a teaspoon of grenadine on top.

Serve and enjoy

Stuffed Chicken Salad Tomatoes

Ingredients:

- 3 small tomatoes
- 1 celery stalk
- 1 cup of smashed avocados
- (Chicken salad)
- 1 cup of cooked chicken breast chopped
- 1 teaspoon of onions chopped
- 1 pinch of black pepper
- 2 tablespoons of mayo
- Mix the chicken into a bowl with onions, mayo and pepper well.

Directions:

1. Cut tomatoes top off.
2. Take a spoon and clean out the insides of the tomatoes.
3. Stuff the inside of the tomato with the chicken salad.
4. Top off the tomato with the smashed avocado.
5. Cut the celery stalks into one inch strips and place them at the bottom of the tomatoes neatly.

Serve and enjoy

Stuffed Egg Avocado Chicken Salad

Ingredients:

- 3 boiled eggs
- 1 cup of smashed avocados
- 1 teaspoon of mayonnaise
- 1 pinch of black pepper
- (Chicken salad)
- 1 cup of cooked chicken breast chopped
- 1 teaspoon of onions chopped
- 1 pinch of black pepper
- 2 tablespoons of mayo
- Mix the chicken into a bowl with onions, mayo and pepper well.

Directions:

Stuffing the Egg

1. Cut the bottom of the egg (so it will sit up) then use a teaspoon to take out the yolk.
2. Stuff the eggs with the chicken salad and neatly put the smashed avocados on top.
3. Garnish with black pepper and enjoy!

Strawberry Shortcake

Ingredients:

- 2 slices of strawberry cake
- 2 scoops of ice cream
- 1 cup of fresh strawberries
- Whipped cream
- Red editable glitter or brew dust
- 2 tablespoons of strawberry syrup
- ¼ cup of granola

Directions:

1. Place 2 slices of strawberry cake on a plate side by side.
2. Add ice cream, strawberries and the strawberry syrup on top.
3. Add granola on top then add whipped cream.
4. Garnish with drizzled strawberry syrup and a French vanilla pirouette stick.

71

Barbie Sundae

Ingredients:

- 4 slices of strawberry cake
- 4 scoops of strawberry ice cream
- 2 tablespoons of strawberry syrup
- 1 teaspoon of editable pink glitter or brew dust
- 4 pink mamba candy stick
- 4 mini strawberry donuts
- Whipped cream

Directions:

1. Place the strawberry cake into a clear container of your choice. You will be creating layers.
2. Start by having three chunks of strawberry cake at the bottom and sides of your bowl.
3. Add a scoop of strawberry ice cream in the center. (this start your first layer)
4. Then add another layer of your strawberry cake.
5. Next layer, add 2 scoops of strawberry ice cream.
6. Add another layer, then add strawberries and strawberry syrup.
7. Then conclude with more strawberries, strawberry syrup and whipped cream.
8. Sprinkle your pink editable glitter or brew dust on top. Then add your mamba candy on each corner and then the strawberry donuts.

73

BBQ Tuna Sandwich

Ingredients:

- 3 Texas toast
- ¼ cup of Jazz Jazz BBQ sauce
- 1 can of tuna
- 1 pinch of black pepper
- 1 teaspoon of mayo (optional)
- 2 slices of tomatoes
- 4 pickles
- 2 lettuce leaf

Directions:

1. Place tuna into a bowl.
2. Add Jazz Jazz BBQ sauce, black pepper and onion.
3. Toast the Texas toast then add mayo, tuna, pickles, lettuce and tomatoes.

Enjoy!

Printed in the USA
CPSIA information can be obtained
at www.ICGtesting.com
LVHW060006260524
781370LV00003B/29